The Ingenious Guide to

Twitter

Steve Eason

Ingenious Internet Income Publishing
www.IngeniousInternetIncome.com

Table of Contents

In today's age, communication has become the number one focus when it comes to technology. In a recent update, the International Telecommunications Union, the United Nations Agency on communication said that there were 6 Billion mobile subscriptions worldwide. That's the equivalent to 87% of the world's population. That's just an amazing number. Needless to say, we love to communicate with friends, with family, with businesses we work with, about our hobbies and about our personal interests no matter where we are.

Back in March of 2006, a small podcasting company had an idea on how they could improve communication and thus Twitter (back then it was first known as twttr) was born. The term Twitter fit the idea that they were looking for. Defined as...

"a short burst of inconsequential information"

it summed up the concept quite nicely. The basis for Twitter was to provide a service similar to SMS, or text messaging. However it also pulled inspiration from a few other sources: instant messaging and blog publishing.

Combining these different ideas, the basic structure that we're familiar with today evolved and it was extremely useful and eventually caught the attention of the world. In 2007, Twitter finally broke into the mainstream in a big way. At the annual South by Southwest Interactive (SXSWi) Conference, Twitter was on location with 2 large plasma screens placed at key locations where they were livestreaming Twitter feeds for the conference. Attendees were able to keep up with the speakers and other conference goers and everyone was talking about it. They ended up winning the festival's

Web Award prize, which they accepted saying...

"We'd like to thank you in 140 characters or less. And we just did".

Fast Forward to the modern day, and you'll find that Twitter has grown by leaps and bounds. With over 500 million active users, Twitter sees more than 340 million tweets and handles over 1.6 billion searches each day. Today it's one of the top 10 most visited websites on the internet. In fact, it's captured the attention of an entire generation. The USA Today reported recently that more and more teens are migrating to Twitter from Facebook. As one teen put it...

"Facebook is like shouting into a crowd. Twitter is like speaking into a room."

One of the biggest issues that new users to Twitter face is understanding how to use the service to their advantage and to reach current and potential customers for their business. In this guide, I'll show you how to setup your Twitter account from scratch, show you how to customize it to match your brand, and how to use it effectively.

Chapter 1: Setting Up An Account

Step 1: Setting it up

Setting up a Twitter account is very easy and fairly straightforward. There isn't much to it. You start by going to www.twitter.com. Once there you will see a screen similar to this one.

Just fill out the information on the bottom right corner and click on Sign Up For Twitter. By the way, the information you enter here can be changed on the next screen.

Step 2: Choosing a Twitter User Name

Once that is completed, you will be brought to a screen where you need to fill out some additional information. When filling out this information there are a few things to consider.

Join Twitter today.

Full name	☒ ✖ A name is required!
Email	☒ ✖ An email is required!
Password	✖ Password must be at least 6 characters.
Username	☒ ✖ A username is required! You can change it later

Suggestions: IncTerry IncHarris inc_terry inc_harris

☑ Keep me signed-in on this computer.

☑ Tailor Twitter based on my recent website visits Learn more

By clicking the button, you agree to the terms below:

These Terms of Service ("Terms") govern your access to and use of the services, including our various websites, SMS, APIs, email notifications,

Printable versions:
Terms of Service · Privacy Policy

Create my account

Note: Others will be able to find you by name, username or email. Your email will not be shown publicly. You can change your privacy settings at any time.

- The Username is limited to 15 characters.

- The Username is not case-senstive. However the name will be saved just how you type it in. For example, if you entered "TwitterUser" you will be listed on Twitter as @TwitterUser, but you can still be found by someone using @twitteruser.

- Keep in mind that a large amount of followers will be using Twitter from mobile devices. By avoiding the use of numbers and other characters like underscores. Because it takes extra steps for mobile users to use those characters, it will make it easier for those users to reach out to you and read your information by not using them.

Should I use my real name or my business name?

This is a common question and one that deserves a little thought. One thing to keep in mind when using Twitter is that most users relate to individuals on the service. They like to communicate with individuals versus businesses. Consider it to be short conversations with your followers. However, that doesn't mean you shouldn't have a Twitter account for your business as well.

Does this mean I have to maintain 2 or more Twitter accounts?

It all depends on your goals, the size of the company and the interaction you expect to have with your followers. Let's look at a few examples that should help you figure out which way to go.

In a business where it's just one person that is the name associated with the company, such as Pat Flynn with Smart Passive Income, you could go either direction. He has chosen to go with his name, because he's looking to create relationships with his followers. By using his name, people feel a sense of connecting on a personal level that changes that relationship. But if he chose to use his business name instead, it wouldn't be a bad thing, but it might put his followers at a different position in the relationship. It can be more impersonal to some people.

However, if you have a larger, recognizable brand or plan to, followers will tend to care less about who is on the other end.

For example, many companies are starting to offer support services through their Twitter account and customers are able to send questions to get answers. Dell offers support through the Twitter account @DellCares. Users can then send a message such as "@ DellCares I have an issue with my laptop. Help!" or they can even promote and talk about favorite products by sending "I love my new @Dell laptop!".

Also keep in mind that if a user is scanning through a large amount of responses, you want your name to stand out in their mind as a trusted resource and authority. Picking something that does that will help get the attention of others.

So depending on your specific situation it may make more sense to choose a personal name or a business name. Either way I recommend registering both of the names so that you can keep others from doing so, especially the business name.

It might mean that you have 2 Twitter accounts, one personal and one business, but you focus on just one of those accounts as your primary route of communicating with followers. I chose to use my business name with my account and I use that one primarily for communicating with followers. My personal account, is just that, personal. I follow friends and interests there and communicate in a different way than I do with my business account. On my business account I keep my content specifically around my niche and I follow other's who do the same.

Should I include keywords in my name?

Yes and no. If you spend any time at all on Twitter just watching, you'll quickly see that those accounts that are often keyword targeted are doing nothing but generating what could be construed as ads or spam. So to avoid a negative connotation, it might be best not to create a keyword focused Twitter user name. But if it's a part of your brand, it would make sense to include that in the name.

Finishing up

From this point forward the Creation Wizard will walk you through several screens where you are encouraged to Follow famous people. I typically will just click on Skip This Step at the bottom of the page and move past these sections completely. I don't want to follow any of those people and I would much rather move on and continue building my profile.

Chapter 2: Setting Up Your Profile

Step 3: Profile Setup

Once you've finished the Creation process, we next need to tailor your Profile. This is VERY important to do. It is what will be displayed to anyone who follows you or is interested in following you. To access the Profile Settings, at the top right hand corner of the page, click on the person icon with the arrow next to it. This brings out the menu. On this menu, click on Settings.

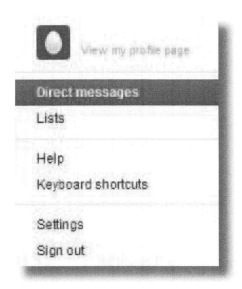

Once you get to the settings page, there are several options listed on the left side of the screen. Where we will be focusing our efforts at is the Profile section. Click on the word Profile to open the profile page.

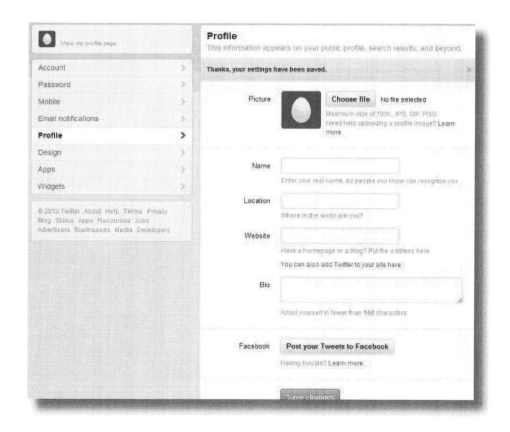

Step 4: Upload your Profile Image

It's extremely important to upload an image to your Twitter profile. You don't want to give the impression that you aren't willing or able to even simply update your Twitter image. This is one of the first things followers will see and you need to create that great first impression. Plus it will help:

- Followers recognize your posts
- Recognition for your brand or face
- Maintain consistency between social platforms. It's a good idea to use the same images across the social platforms.

As we mentioned earlier, Twitter is typically seen as a personal approach, so it's a good idea to avoid using company logos as your profile image, unless you are focused on your brand. Even though I'm using my business name for my Twitter account, I have used a personal image so that my followers recognize my face and it changes our relationship to a more personal level.

A few tips on choosing an image to use as a profile picture.

1. Use a friendly image of yourself. Remember that it's like having a conversation with another person. If the image on their profile is unfriendly, it doesn't create a positive feeling for the other individual.

2. Focus on leaving a positive impression. Don't use an image that you took when you woke up this morning. Images like that can leave the impression that you might be disorganized, lazy or another unfavorable idea, especially if you want people to buy something from you.

3. One of the biggest reasons I recommend not to use a logo is that *people buy from other people*. Again that dreaded word, relationships. You're trying to create a relationship and people don't build relationships with business.

4. Avoid wearing dark glasses. It puts a barrier between you and your followers. One of the best ways to communicate with another individual is through eye-contact. It sounds silly, but you want to have eye contact with your followers.

5. It's ok to show your personality in your image. If you are fun and easy going, show that in your image. But don't go too far overboard, just be natural.

Step 5: Add a link to your website

Unfortunately you only are able to add one website link to your profile, so you want to make sure it's pointing to your best location for people to find more about you. In almost all cases, you want this to be your primary website or blog. However, you might consider setting up a Twitter Landing page on your website.

Step 6: Setup A Twitter Landing Page On Your Site

Now, one thing I have seen done is creating a special landing page for your followers to go to when they click on your link. A really good example of this is from @CindyKing. Her landing page for Twitter followers (http://cindyking.biz/resources/twitter/) that list out people she recommends others follow that are categorized into groups. Plus she shares other ways to keep in touch with her.

Another great example is Darren Rowse (@ProBlogger). His landing page (http://www.problogger.net/about-darren-rowse-problogger/) tells more about him and about the services he offers, his books and other information that might interest visitors.

These landing pages provide you an opportunity to personally connect with your followers in an unexpected way. It's not just a link to their primary website, but a link to a page that is specifically focusing on establishing a relationship, there is that word again, with your followers. You took the time to not only recognize that they were coming to visit, but you wanted to share specific information with them about who you are, what they can find on your site and even leads to other people that they might find informative and worth checking out. It's a big hug to a visitor when they cross your doorstep.

Additionally when a visitor clicks on your Twitter profile, they are looking to find out more information about you. They want to know more about the individual and how to connect with them. By pointing them to a custom tailored Twitter landing page, you can quickly answer those questions that they might have and give them what is known as a call to action. Give them a little background about you, tell them about your products and encourage them to follow you, sign up for your mailing list or purchase your products. Think outside of the box and be creative, but keep in mind the thoughts above.

Step 7: Uploading a Header Image

Twitter has just added the ability to upload a header image to your profile. This is very similar to what you will find on Facebook with their Timeline feature. The sizing is a little different from Facebook, so here are the dimension requirements.

· Minimum of 1252 x 626 in size
· Maximum file size of 5 MB
· When you upload the image, it's placed at the top of your profile page and they superimpose your information over the image.

I would recommend that you create your image to avoid placing anything in the middle of the image, because as you can see in my example, it's going to be covered by your title, text and link.

To upload your image, simply click on the Gear icon at the top right corner of your Twitter page, and click on Settings. When on the Settings page, on the left side click on Design, and just below the Theme selection area, is the option to upload your Header image. You will be given the opportunity to adjust the size of the image and the positioning prior to saving the image.

Word Of Warning

I must take a moment and issue a word of warning. I have heard about some people taking creativity a little too far. If you notice in the Ryan Seacrest example above, he has a blue check mark next to his name. This badge means that Twitter has officially confirmed his account. Twitter doesn't do this for the general public, but they are doing it for popular individuals in several categories, such as music, acting, fashion, government, religion, journalism, etc. In order to get the badge, you have to fall into one of those categories and have been contacted by Twitter directly. You cannot request to have your account verified and get the badge.

Now, with the implementation of the Header Image, some people have figured out that if you add the check badge into your image, placed just right it looks like you have a badge on your account. As much as this seems like a fun idea, be sure to check out the Twitter Rules, especially this part:

"Misuse of Twitter Badges: You may not use a Verified Account badge or Promoted Products badge unless it is provided by Twitter. Accounts using these badges as part of profile photos, header photos, background images, or in a way that falsely implies affiliation with Twitter will be suspended."

So, if you don't want to get BANNED, don't use the Twitter badge in your images. Other than that, from what I can tell, you can do pretty much what you want to with the image. I suspect that this will change in the near future once some creative individuals find ways to abuse this option. But for now, go out there and have some fun. But keep the guidelines in mind before you have too much fun.

Step 8: Create an Interesting Bio

Your Twitter Bio is where you get to let your potential followers learn a little bit about you. The only issue is that you only have 160 characters in which to make this happen. The key to writing a good or even great bio is asking yourself the following question.

"Will someone reading my bio want to follow me?"

Have you provided them with enough reasons of why you might be worth following? Given the limited amount of space there are a few tips I would recommend considering when creating your bio.

1. Include keywords – yes, this is a great place to include keywords for your niche. Google does index these bio boxes and this will help people find you and follow you.

2. Don't stuff the bio – As the item before said, you can add keywords, but don't stuff the bio full of nothing but keywords. Remember, the key here is that we're building relationships.

3. Watch your grammar and spelling – Make sure you use proper spelling in your bio. Again this is part of the first impression and a box full of misspelled words is NOT a good impression.

4. How you can help – Tell your followers how you can help them. Let them know what it is you are good at. Let them know what you want to teach them or share with them.

5. Don't copy others – It's best to be unique and come up with your own bio. It's frowned upon to copy other users bios.

6. Be Interesting and Engaging - If you create an interesting, engaging bio, you are bound to attract similar thinking people and really connect on a personal level. Spend a few minutes really thinking it through and then execute it. It will be worth your time.

Chapter 3: Designing Your Profile Page

Step 9: Designing Your Profile Page

On the next page of the Settings area is where you can choose a background for your Twitter Profile page. Twitter provides a few options for you of premade themes, but there isn't anything special found here that will let you stand out from the rest of the crowd. I highly recommend that you customize your background so that you are unique and display something that starts the relationship building process.

There are really 3 types of designs that are the most commonly found among Twitter users, other than just choosing the default templates or a plain color.

Repeating Background Pattern

Reaching back into the old days of plain old HTML websites, some people will use what are called seamless images to place a pattern across the full page. The advantage to this is that it will be the same for any user no matter what size monitor they are using.

Here are some examples:

Image fading to color

Another option is to use an image, usually centered on the top left corner or along the left side of the screen. Then take that image and either fade it out as it moves across the screen to a color you can choose as the background color in your Twitter Profile.

Here are some examples:

27

Extra large background image

The last option is using a really large background image that fills the entire screen. This does really ramp up the creative side and effect however, there will be issues where some screens just can display all of the image. You have to consider smaller resolution screens when choosing this options.

Here are some examples:

Should I include a sidebar?

What I've seen with both the Image fading to color and extra large background image options is some users utilizing a sidebar to display more information about how you can reach them or other content. The background image doesn't allow any type of link to be included but if you have your website address listed along with other ways to reach you, the user could then manually type it in and find you. I personally like this option and even more I like it when it's done creatively.

Here are some examples:

There are all kinds of ways you can use the space around your Twitter page. Try to think differently. Do a search on Google and look at custom Twitter backgrounds for inspiration. There are numerous sites out there that have lots of examples to ooh and aww over.

Chapter 4: Basics of Using Twitter

We've talked all about signing up and creating your account, how to create a bio page, using #hashtags and more, but the one thing we haven't really talked about is how to use Twitter itself. Let's take a few minutes to look at some of the features you should know about.

140 Character Limitation

Yes you are limited to only 140 characters in each of your posts. But don't look at this as a limitation. In fact you really shouldn't even be using 140 characters. If at all possible, try to limit yourself to 120 characters or less so that your followers can comment on your post when they retweet it. You will be surprised at how much you can fit into a short statement.

But, that is the point with Twitter. The idea is to carefully consider what you want to say and to say it efficiently without unnecessary words. Worst case scenario, say it over multiple posts. But it's a good idea to include a #hashtag if you do.

Learning the Twitter Language

If you have looked around in Twitter at all, you might have noticed that there are a few commonly used terms that have special meanings. It's really important that you understand what all these terms mean before you venture out into that strange new world. I've listed out a few that you should know below.

Tweet – This is what a post is called on Twitter. For example, "I just sent out a tweet to my friends." Some people might also call it "twits", but a "tweet" is the official term.

@ (The @ symbol) – Twitter uses the @ symbol to refer to another user. So if you type in your Tweet, @IngeniousIncome, you are either sending a message specifically to that person or you are talking about them in your message. On the Twitter homepage, you can find at the top of the screen, the menu item @Connect. This will show you anyone or anytime someone has included your Twitter name in a message using the @ symbol.

Retweet or RT – The retweet is when you share something you received from another Twitter user to your followers. When you retweet something, it's customary to include "RT @username" at the beginning of the post, so that others know that it originally came from the person listed. It might look like this. "RT @IngeniousIncome We hit 1,000 followers!". In this example, you are retweeting the message that IngeniousIncome sent out about hitting 1,000 followers. I should note that it's considered to be a bad idea to retweet someone and not include a credit to them for it.

Direct Message or DM – A direct message is just that, a message directly to an individual. This is not a public message and only to that specific account. However, you can only DM to someone who is following you. To DM, all you have to do is start your message with "DM Username" or "DM IngeniousIncome".

Reply or @Reply – A response to a Tweet, is generally called a Reply. This is a public message and Twitter will automatically append the original users name as such "@Username".

Mention – If you use the @Username in the body of your Tweet, your message will go out to those people who follow you and this is called a "mention". This is different than a DM (Direct Message) in that it's not limited to just that individual. Plus a DM requires that the @Username is at the beginning of the post.

Follower – A follower is a person who has subscribed to your Tweets. They are following your posts and usually are interested in what you have to say. The biggest difference between Facebook and Twitter is that this relationship is a one-way relationship. One doesn't have to follow people who are following them. However, often times others will follow you if you follow them.

Hashtag or # - This is one of the most used functions found on Twitter. The Hashtag (#) is used when a group of people are talking about a specific event or topic. For example, during the Olympics, when anyone was discussing or referencing the games, they could include the #Olympics in their post and anyone who was following that particular hashtag would see the message. You can search for specific hashtags by entering #Name in the Twitter search bar at the top of the page. You can also look at the Trending Topics to see what subjects are the most popular. These often include hashtags that are popular at that moment.

Trending – When a subject or term is extremely popular on Twitter, it's often referred to as a "Trending Topic". On Twitter's page, you can see a listing of the current Trending Topics on the left side of your screen. This list of trends changes all the time and topics can come and go in a matter of hours if not minutes. During major events, such as natural disasters, sporting events, television shows or even just big news stories, you will see the topics change to reflect what is being talked about the most.

Bookmark Tweets For Review Later

Something else I learned while digging into Twitter was that each tweet has its own web address! If you want to bookmark a tweet (in your web browser's bookmarks), just click on the word Expand at the bottom of the specific tweet you want to save.

Ingenious Income @ingeniousincome
Thought I'd go back to the basics: Domains and Hosting - ingeniousinternetincome.com/back-to-the-ba...
Expand

Once you expand out the post you will see another option below that that says Details. Click on Details and that will bring you to the webpage for that specific tweet, which you can then bookmark for later review.

Ingenious Income @ingeniousincome
Thought I'd go back to the basics: Domains and Hosting - ingeniousinternetincome.com/back-to-the-ba...
Collapse ← Reply 🗑 Delete ★ Favorite

9:35 AM - 17 Sep 12 · Details

Marking Favorites in Twitter

You might have noticed a few other options when you hovered over the Expand option on a tweet. One of those options was Favorite. This is often used to mark inside Twitter a post that you would like to access later. It also lets the original poster, know that you liked their tweet.

If you want to view the tweets that you have marked, just below your name on your home page, there is an option to open your profile page. On your profile page, you will see in the menu the option to view your favorites.

You can also view other users' favorites by visiting their profile page and finding their favorites in the same location. Keep in mind that if a user with protected tweets is listed as a favorite, only the users who are actual followers of that user can see the post.

Creating Lists

Lists are a great way to organize your tweets and conversations in Twitter. The idea behind lists is that you can group certain people you follow into groups however you like to organize them. When you view a list timeline, you will see only tweets coming from those people on your list. The list only pertains to what you are reading, so you cannot respond to just a list of users. But it is a great way to organize your account into easily digested segments that make more sense.

To create a list, go to your Lists Page, which you can get to by clicking on the Person icon on the top right corner, and then clicking Lists. Click on Create List, name the list and give it a description and then decide if you want it to be a private or public list. Once done, Save List.

Once you have a list created, if you visit someone else's profile you can add them to your list. Just click on their Person drop-down menu and click on Add or remove from lists. You can add anyone you like even if you are not a follower. Choose which list to add that user to or remove from and you're finished.

You can also view other people's lists if they marked them public. This gives you the ability to quickly find interesting people that you could follow in the future. Again, even if you are following people via a list, you don't have to be following those people individually.

If you want to see lists that you are on, go to your lists page and click on Member of. This will show you what lists you are on.

You can create up to 20 different Twitter lists and you have up to 500 accounts on each list.

Organization of Tweets

The original purpose of the #hashtag was for users to be able to group their posts into understandable subjects so that they can find the information at a later date. By using #hashtags in your posts, it will help you find information in the future.

So there are many different things you can use #hashtags for and it amazed me that someone has actually spent the time to create a huge spreadsheet to track all those different conversations that are happening each week. Don't be afraid to experiment and to participate in those conversations. The more you participate and add valuable information, the more likely you might pick up a few new followers who turn into customers.

Hashtag (#) Conversations

There are so many conversations happening on Twitter each and every day, it would be extremely difficult to track, view or follow them without hashtags. Hashtags are extremely useful and are a great way to organize your daily interactions. I want to look at the ways you can use hashtags in your Twitter conversations to enhance your online experience with Twitter.

Archiving Posts

One way to utilize hashtags is to archive your whole conversation for use at a later date. This could be compiling the information to create an ebook or just saving the conversation for those involved to review at a later time. If you include a #hashtag with your posts, you can pull them all up at a later time quickly and easily for review.

Tracking Conversations

Add a #hashtag to a conversation to allow you to see what others had to contribute to the conversation. It's similar to the Archiving discussion above, but the purpose is different.

Host a Twitter Chat with a hashtag

Something that I really didn't even know existed until I started digging even deeper into Twitter, was that there are lots of ongoing Twitter chats happening each and every week around just about any topic. All you need to know to find them is the #hashtag to get started. And to help that process, there is a Google Spreadsheet that has hundreds of them listed to get you started. Most of these Twitter chats are scheduled events and are recurring. They also often have a moderator to keep the conversation on topic.

You can find the spreadsheet by using this URL:

Google Spreadsheet - Twitter Chats
http://www.ingeniousinternetincome.com/TwitterChatSchedule

You can start your own by promoting it through your followers or your website. Just choose a #hashtag and start posting. Anyone who wants to join in on that conversation can do so just by searching for the #hashtag on the Twitter main page. When creating your own Twitter chat, it's a good idea to focus the chat around an existing issue or topic. Also be sure to set some ground rules so that participants will know what you expect. Have a list of questions or discussion starters ready ahead of time and try to limit the chat to a specific period of time.

Chapter 5: What And When Do I Tweet?

What Do I Tweet?

Now that you have your Twitter account all setup and you're ready to post, what do you post about? Well the answer is easier than you think. Let's look at a few suggestions.

Tweet What You Know

You should write about what you know. Don't post about fly fishing and knitting when you don't know anything about it. Write posts that you have a lot of knowledge about and what you have a passion for. Even though it's only 140 characters, if it's something that you're passionate about, it will be reflected in your posts.

Be Interesting

You will find that being interesting and entertaining will go a long way for you on Twitter. People love to be entertained online. Be creative and have a little fun with your posts and you'll find that you grow followers naturally.

Link To Interesting Stuff

Find interesting things that your followers would like to see. You will know when you hit the right buttons with your followers when they reply, retweet or direct message you with thanks. Sure it's ok to link to your own stuff once in a while, but a majority of the time it should be elsewhere.

Ask and Answer Questions

In an effort to engage your followers, ask questions. Just throw an idea out there. The idea is to generate some conversations. Send a question to someone you are following about one of their recent tweets.

Share Other's Tweets

If someone sends out something that you like, retweet it. You'll find on Twitter that it's more likely to help you later on. That's what Twitter is all about.

Use Images

Frequently include images in your tweets. People like to look at images and they will often retweet them.

Reveal Yourself

Twitter is a place where you can relax and be yourself, to an extent. It's more personable and people like to get to know you better through more personal updates. But not too personal.

Mix It Up

Mix up your posts, so that they include a little bit of each of the above suggestions and more. The idea is to keep things interesting. If you are constantly doing the same thing over and over, you're likely to lose followers. Spread out the love.

This isn't all you can write about, but it should get you started. Take some time to find people in your niche and see what they write about.

Knowing When To Post

Another great piece of information is knowing when your followers are often online and seeing your posts. If you target the time when most of your followers are online, you will get the most impact from your posts. Tweriod organizes all your followers' timezone information and lets you know when the best time to tweet them is. This will help you get in front of your followers when they are online.

Knowing Which Links Get Retweeted

If you use a URL shortener to track your links, you can get a rough idea of which ones are being retweeted the most. If you know which content is getting the most traction with your followers, you can then focus on more of that same content. In fact if you want to get your tweets retweeted, try including some of the following posts.

- Controversial stories or topics
- Inspiring quotes
- Humor
- Breaking news

By including some of those ideas in your tweets, you're likely to get more of those posts retweeted. Be creative, track the results and find out what works best with your audience.

Chapter 6: Know How You Use Twitter

Knowing how you are already using Twitter helps you adjust your process. There is a great site, TweetStats, where you can enter your Twitter user name and it will graph out which hours, days and months you tweet the most. It also displays numerous other bits o information that can be helpful.

Setting Goals and Objectives

When starting to use Twitter, you really need to understand what i is that you want to get out of Twitter in the first place. By setting out a list of goals and objectives that you want to achieve, it helps define and direct how and what you post on Twitter. So take a mo ment to really think about this question.

What do you want to achieve with Twitter?

Seriously. Grab a pen and paper and just take a few minutes to write down a few ideas of what you want to achieve. This is a brainstorming exercise, so don't try to do anything other than jot down a bunch of ideas. I'll wait for you.

If you need some help here, I have a few suggestions you could use to get you started:

- I want to promote my brand
- I want to be known as the authority in my niche
- I want to drive traffic to my website
- I want to find new customers

- I want to find new readers
- I want to share my passion for (insert niche here)
- I want to establish new friendships who are interested in what I like

You might have a much longer list than this when you are done, but once you finish the little exercise, take another moment and prioritize this list into the primary things you want to accomplish using Twitter.

When you have the list sorted, try to narrow the list down to just 2-3 of the items that are the most important. This is what you need to focus on the most when using Twitter. You can always refine this list later on, but you really should focus on these key elements at the beginning.

Now that you have a short list of objectives, use them to help guide and direct your activity on Twitter. By keeping this in focus you will start to find out that:

- Your tweets will be more focused
- Who you follow and interact with will make more sense
- Your content will reach more people

It's good to keep focused because you can become easily distracted when trying to do too much at the same time. This is also a great time for me to mention that as with everything that I do with my blog and by interacting with my readers, Twitter is no different. It's about creating a relationship that helps my readers connect with me in a meaningful way.

URL Shorteners

You might have come across a URL shortener at some point while surfing the internet. What URL shortener does is it shortens URL' to more manageable length, that make it easier to use in services such as Twitter. You can easily take a 40-100 character long URL (website address) into a 20 character link. Additionally, most of the URL shorteners available will track the number of clicks that each shortened URL receives for you to analyze at a later date.

There are a quite a few different services available that do this and the question has always been which one do you use. Well I've narrowed down my list to just three that I feel are your best options.

Bit.ly

Bit.ly is probably the most popular of the services available. Some of it's better features are real-time stats (just add a "+" sign at the end of the link to get real time stats), No account required, customizable links, if you have an account you can archive your links and you can upgrade to their paid service to get even more features.

Goo.gl

This service is provided by Google. It's not quite as popular and many people shy away from it because it's offered by Google. But at the same time, one of the reasons I'm considering using it more is that it's possible that the links you create with the service could be factored into Google's overall search engine algorithm. Just like

Bit.ly, they have detailed analytics, it creates automatic QR codes and they spam filter the links to keep things clean and safe.

T.co

T.co is Twitter's own version of a URL shortener. You cannot use the service anywhere but on Twitter and the way you create a link is just by pasting a long link into your Twitter post. If the post is too long, Twitter will automatically shorten it down to 20 characters. The nice part about this option is that it's easy to use and you don't have to go outside of the site to use it. However, you can't check the analytics with this service.

I do recommend that you use a URL shortener when posting links for the analytics if nothing else. Knowing which of your links are getting the most clicks really helps you understand your audience better.

Who Do I Follow?

One of the best ways to start out is to find someone you know and trust to follow. Having a starting point helps get the ball rolling. Once you have one or two that you're following, look and see who they are following. There is a high probability that they are following some interesting people.

Another great trick I've heard of is asking another Twitter user to introduce you to their network. That could open up the door to some new followers and you move on from there.

Look at other users' lists. There are some great lists out there depending on what niche you are in. You can search on Google for Twitter Lists and you'll find lots of lists that come highly recommended.

#FollowFriday is what you could call an activity where people make recommendations on people to follow every Friday. If you want to see the recommendations, search on Twitter for either Follow Friday or #followfriday.

If you have a few blogs you enjoy, go check the site to see if they have a Twitter link to their account. Follow them and then check to see who they follow. It's a great way to build a list from those in subjects that interest you.

Do a keyword search on Twitter around subjects that interest you and see who's talking about it. Read more about those people and consider following them. Then after that see who they are following.

Before you know it you'll have quite a list built up of people you are following. And quite naturally you should start seeing people following you as they discover you and what you are about.

Chapter 7: Searching And Tracking

Searching Twitter

One of the great things about Twitter is that EVERYTHING is searchable. If you want to find any information at all on Twitter, just use their built in search box at the top. You can search by keywords, user names or #hashtags. Additionally, you can narrow that search down to the top tweets with those words, all the tweets or just those from people you follow. But unfortunately, even using that search feature won't help you find exactly what you need every time. Thankfully there are numerous search tools available online to help with that. We'll look at a few of those tools here:

Backtweets (www.backtweets.com) – This is a pretty amazing tool. With this tool you can search for links and shortened URL's on Twitter. If someone shared a link, you can find it even if it was shortened by a URL shortener.

Nearby Tweets (www.nearbytweets.com) – Using Google Maps, this site finds your location and then shows tweets from other Twitter users nearby. It's a great way to find out what people in your area are talking about.

Local Follow (www.localfollow.com) – This search tool allows you to search users through 4 main search fields – Bio, Location, Name and Tweets. Using the Twitter API, it can search and produce results based on your keywords.

Snapbird (www.snapbird.org) – Allows you to search your friends tweets, direct messages you sent or within any user's favorites. Plus it lets you go back more than 10 days.

Topsy (www.topsy.com) – This search engine follows conversations around the web to show you what everyone is talking about. You can search and find all kinds of information plus they have analytics to show you trends.

Twellow (www.twellow.com) – Often called the Yellow Pages of Twitter. What they've done is taken the information that they collect about Twitter users and organize the information in a yellow pages format. You can search for services, people in different professions and a lot more.

Twitjobsearch (www.twitjobsearch.com) – Looking for a job? This tool filters out tweets that include the words like "hiring", "job", etc. Pretty cool tool.

As you can see there are many ways to search through the data contained on Twitter. You're sure to find what you need with one of those tools above.

Twitter Metrics – Tracking and Analysis

In order to be the most effective you can be on Twitter, it's important that you track your progress. Tracking your progress is more than just knowing how many followers you have. Anyone can get a large amount of followers in a short period of time. The important numbers are some of the following:

Influence Factor

Whether you have 50 followers or 50,000 the more important number is how many of those people who are following you actually listening. Of course this is a difficult number to track but there are a few tools out there that will help.

Klout (www.klout.com) is one of the tools that is gaining the biggest following. What Klout does is takes all your different social media accounts and incorporates about 400 different signals from those different networks and generates your Klout score. This score is an indicator of how influential you are to you audience.

Another site is **Peerindex (www.peerindex.com)**. This is very similar to Klout and they have different signals that they incorporate to come up with your Peerindex score.

If you work at building your scores on both of those sites, you will become a more effective influencer.

We've covered a wide array of topics throughout this guide and I hope that you've found loads of information that you can take action on. Twitter is an extremely deep site and can be a incredible boost to your business if used correctly.

I wish the best for you and your business.

Steve Eason
Ingenious Internet Income

Questions or Comments?

I'd love to hear your thoughts. Email me at: steve@ingeniousinternetincome.com

Need Help?

I am constantly adding new training articles and information on my site and I'd be more than happy to help you should you need it. Either contact me via email at **steve@ingeniousinternetincome.com** or visit my site - **www.ingeniousinternetincome.com**.

You can also find me on Twitter **@IngeniousIncome**

Printed in Great Britain
by Amazon